GOAL SETTING FOR A RENEWED YOU

BECAUSE YOU DESERVE IT!
~LISA M BUSKE~

ISBN-13:
978-0692628355 (Lisa M. Buske)

ISBN-10:
0692628355

Published April 3, 2016

INTRODUCTION

Goal setting isn't something new, especially to me. It might be the first born in me, genetic, or my love of lists but regardless of its root...I enjoy setting goals and determining a path to reach them.

I am a third generation list maker, and crosser-off-er-er. Yes, I just made a new word, lol. There is great personal satisfaction when you achieve your goals. In order to achieve a goal though, you first must set it. Some spend time determining and setting one or two goals each year. Me, on the other hand, I tend to be a bit "over the top" as my daughter says. I like to think of myself as a goal setting-organizationalist, with an action plan for success. Sounds official, don't you think?

Once you delve into this book of *Goal Setting for a Renewed You: Because You Deserve It*, you will realize the importance and simplicity of setting achievable goals with a plan for success. My husband and I are on opposite sides of the globe sometimes when it comes to the goal setting process. Maybe it's the polar oppositeness of our birth orders or some unconscious programming within, but this is why our marriage, and goal setting works. We are different individuals so we need different paths for success. He keeps my feet and aspirations closer to the ground while I spur him on to strive for the things he's yet to dream. It's a nice balance.

Why do I share this with you? Simple, this book is not written and designed for every person. You might open it up and spend the weekend and the next week filling in the pages and utilizing every bit of white space. On the other hand, you may look at this book, shake your head and think I'm nuts. Guess what? You are both right! If this isn't your style for goal setting, I hope you will spend some time finding out what works best for you and start setting goals, in writing, for the renewed you. The YOU, you deserve to be!

A quote often repeated when discussing goals is this, *"Goals not written down are only a dream."* To the best of my knowledge, no one knows who first said this and it's a shame because so many repeat it. There is a wealth of truth in these eight words. Many goal setting, inspirational speakers for personal or business growth reference this quote often and encourage their audience to write at least one goal before they leave the conference or workshop.

The first time I did this at a conference, it was hard. People were talking and brainstorming why they needed a particular goal. I found myself second guessing my initial goal, "Do I want to be an entrepreneur? If yes, what do I need to do first?" As I listened to the driven people around me, I felt inadequate and simply wrote a goal that "sounded good" to share when we went around the table. I don't even remember what the goal was but in my heart, my goals were more parenting driven, yet I let peer pressure alter my thoughts.

For this reason, I encourage you to spend time with YOU, no one else. This requires turning off your phone, disconnecting from the Internet, and putting yourself first. This will be difficult yet so important BUT the more you do this, the easier it will be. Get to know yourself, you are worth it.

The first step is to think about what and who is important to you and the areas of your life you want to focus on. What are your strengths? Where are your weaknesses? If you could set any goal, with no limitations, what is the one thing you would write down? Write it now. Don't wait. Don't overthink, just write it down.

~ Table of Contents ~

Congratulations!

Below, write down the one thing in your life that weighs you down. You know what I'm talking about, the one thing you are thinking about when you close your eyes and remains on your heart when you wake up. Don't worry about making it look pretty or punctuation, just write it down. Go "One thing I always say I'd like to change is _____.

This wasn't too difficult, right? So, let's not stop there, will you go a step further? What is the first thing you can do, to change the way this effects your daily living? No negativity.

If finances, time, or health didn't limit you, what can you do to start making a change in this one area? Examples: Be more positive when "x" happens, go back to school, learn a new skill?

_____

_____

_____

_____

What time frame is realistic? One week? Month? Year? 5 Years? _____

_____

_____

Guess what? You just wrote your first goal! You can do this!

*Congratulations,
You've written your 1st Goal!*

Where do you

see yourself in...

The next few pages will challenge you to look into the future.
It starts easy, where do you see yourself next week?
For most, this is an easy answer yet for others,
due to life's circumstances, this might require thought.

I encourage you to complete this look ahead
because it will help you prioritize what and who is important
and where you see yourself down the road.

This process might seem tedious but it will provide clarity and direction
for you in preparation for the journey of goal setting ahead.
If this is overwhelming, start with the "One Week" and
come back to the others as you are more
comfortable with the goal setting process.

~ Notes ~

One Week...

What is one thing you would like to see done or finished at this time next week? _____

_____

_____

Where will you "hang your hat", live? Be as vague or specific as you are comfortable with: __

_____

_____

Is there something you need done by next week in order to reach a different or long term goal? How will doing "x" help you reach this more distant goal? What is "x"? _____

_____

_____

What is one thing you would like to do next week, if there were no obstacles? _____

_____

_____

_____

What stops you from reaching for this goal? _____

_____

Is there something you can do today to help you finish the thing you just mentioned or prepare for a transition to a new location? _____

_____

_____

Who could you ask to be your accountability partner this week to accomplish one, or a few of these things? _____

_____

~ Notes ~

One Month...

What is one thing you would like to see done or finished at this time next month? _____

_____

_____

Where will you "hang your hat", live? Be as vague or specific as you are comfortable with: ___

_____

_____

Is there something you need done by next month in order to reach a different or long term goal? How will doing "x" help you reach this more distant goal? What is "x"? _____

_____

_____

What is one thing you would like to do next month, if there were no obstacles? _____

_____

_____

_____

What stops you from reaching for this goal? _____

_____

Is there something you can do today to help you finish the thing you just mentioned or prepare for a transition to a new location? _____

_____

_____

Who could you ask to be your accountability partner this month to accomplish one, or possible a few of these things? _____

_____

~ Notes ~

One Year...

What is one thing you would like to see done or finished at this time next year? _____

_____

_____

Where will you "hang your hat", live? Be as vague or specific as you are comfortable with: ___

_____

_____

Is there something you need done by next year in order to reach a different or long term goal? How will doing "x" help you reach this more distant goal? What is "x"? _____

_____

_____

What is one thing you would like to do next year, if there were no obstacles? _____

_____

_____

_____

What stops you from reaching for this goal? _____

_____

Is there something you can do today to help you finish the thing you just mentioned or prepare for a transition to a new location? _____

_____

_____

Who could you ask to be your accountability partner this year to accomplish one, or a few of these things? _____

_____

~ Notes ~

Five Years...

What is one thing you would like to see done or finished five years from now? _____
_____
_____

Where will you "hang your hat", live? Be as vague or specific as you are comfortable with: ___
_____
_____

Is there something you need done this year in order to reach this five year goal? How will doing "x" help you reach this more distant goal? What is "x"? _____
_____
_____

What is one thing you would like to do in five years, if there were no obstacles? _____
_____
_____
_____

What stops you from striving to reach this goal? _____
_____

Is there something you can do today to help you finish the thing you just mentioned to prepare for the transition necessary for this to become a reality? _____
_____
_____

Who could you ask to be your accountability partner over the next few years, encouraging you to accomplish these things? _____

~ Notes ~

Ten Years...

What is one thing you would like to see done or finished ten years from now? _____

_____

_____

Where will you "hang your hat", live? Be as vague or specific as you are comfortable with: ___

_____

_____

Is there something you need done this year in order to reach your ten year goal? How will doing "x" help you reach this more distant goal? What is "x"? _____

_____

_____

What is one thing you would like to do in ten years, if there were no obstacles? _____

_____

_____

_____

What stops you from striving to reach this goal? _____

_____

Is there something you can do today to help you finish the thing you just mentioned to prepare for the transition necessary for this to become a reality? _____

_____

_____

Who could you ask to be your accountability partner over the next few years, encouraging you to accomplish these things? _____

Congratulations...

You are ready!

~ A Few Pointers For Successful Goal Writing ~

- **Let It Out:** If you are like me, and want to keep the goal page clean and pristine, use the white space on the neighboring page to organize your thoughts before committing them to a neatly written statement on the goal page.

- **Be Clear and Concise When Writing Your Goals:** It's easier to achieve your goal when you can revisit it with ease and clarity.

- **Set Bold and Brave Goals:** Don't limit yourself or avoid putting a dream into writing and making it a goal because you don't *think* you can achieve it. Take a chance, what is the worst thing to happen...you don't reach the goal or possibly realize there was a different goal to strive for. Sounds like a win-win to me.

- **Determine An Achievable Number of Goals:** You might be a one-at-a-time goal setter or an over achiever, like me, but regardless of your preference, it's important to figure out what works for you. This journal is meant to guide you through the process and get you started.

- **START WHERE YOU ARE COMFORTABLE:** There isn't a traditional *Table of Contents* in this book. The *Goal Setting Target Areas* page, allows you the freedom to choose your starting point. To help you stay motivated, I encourage you to set goals in the area that speaks to you the most. Once those goals are written down, move to another section. The number of goals and the pace at which you determine them is decided by you.

- **MY STARTING POINT:** The goal areas are presented in the order I set my goals. You don't have to follow my direction yet I encourage you to start with your spiritual goals, as these help you stay the course with all your goal setting.

- **DON'T GET OVERWHELMED:** You can do this, one goal at a time!

~ HOW TO WRITE A GOAL & A SAMPLE ~

For a more detailed goal, state your goal like a mission statement
on the top of the page, with mini-goals below it.
This helps to keep you on task and reach your goals.

Sample Mission Statement & Goal Outline

I will infuse prayer into my life throughout the day, so prayer is like breathing...constant.

1) Read the Bible cover to cover using the VOICE version

a. Start no later than January 10th, 2016.

b. See Schedule below: 1,664 pages in total divided by 355 days (starting on January 10th, not the 1st) = 4. 7, rounded up to 5 pages a day

Mini Goal

❖ *Mini Goal #1:* _____

_____

○ _____

_____

○ _____

_____

Steps to help you reach each this goal

*If you need more room to work on your goals, I've included many note pages throughout the book for your convenience. Doodle, note when you achieve a goal, or keep track of what worked and what didn't.

Spiritual

Goals

~ Spiritual Goals Note Page~

~ SPIRITUAL ~

MAIN GOAL (Mission Statement): _____

_____

_____

❖ *Determine Word for the Year*

- ○ Choose a word to encourage you throughout the year, a gentle reminder when you see, hear, or read it of who you want to be or how you want to feel. What is this word? _____

  _____

- ○ My Word for this year is: _____

- ○ WORD FOR THE YEAR: _____

❖ *Determine Scripture Verse for the Year*

- ○ I spend time in prayer and Bible study for a verse that "speaks to me" when I read it. Sometimes I don't understand why a particular verse stands out until later in the year and I'm thankful this verse is a part of my day, reminding me of God's love and presence in my life. _____

- ○ Old Testament or New Testament? _____

- ○ Book of the Bible you are called to? _____

- ○ A theme that stands out to you? _____

- ○ Will your Bible verse relate to your Word for the year? _____

- ○ What verse did you choose? _____

- ○ SCRIPTURE VERSE FOR THE YEAR: _____

~ Spiritual Goals Note Page~

Time to set your spiritual mini-goals. These will help you achieve your main goal, with ways to accomplish each mini goal. Mini goals will help you feel the success of your hard work, in the midst of striving towards your main goal.

❖ *Mini Goal #1:* _____

_____

    ○ _____

_____

    ○ _____

_____

❖ *Mini Goal #2:* _____

_____

    ○ _____

_____

    ○ _____

_____

❖ *Mini Goal #3:* _____

_____

    ○ _____

_____

    ○ _____

_____

Health &
Fitness Goals

~ Health & Fitness Goals Note Page ~

~ Health & Fitness Goals ~

MAIN GOAL (Mission Statement): _____

_____

_____

_____

❖ *When you look in the mirror, what do you see? What is the first thing you notice that discourages you? List it, or them, here:* _____

_____

_____

_____

❖ *Now, be honest, is this something YOU can change?* _____

❖ *If not, then, what will help you accept yourself as the unique and beautiful individual God created you to be?* _____

_____

_____

❖ *If it's something you CAN change, where do you want to begin? What area will you target first? Why?* _____

_____

_____

_____

❖ Is there someone you trust to share your health and fitness goals with? An accountability partner increases your success.

~ Health & Fitness Goals Note Page ~

Time to set your health and fitness mini-goals. These will help you achieve your main goal, with ways to accomplish each mini goal. Mini goals will help you feel the success of your hard work, in the midst of striving towards your main goal.

❖ Mini Goal #1: _____

_____

    ○ _____

_____

    ○ _____

_____

❖ Mini Goal #2: _____

_____

    ○ _____

_____

    ○ _____

_____

❖ Mini Goal #3: _____

_____

    ○ _____

_____

    ○ _____

_____

~ Health & Fitness Goals Note Page ~

Time to set your health and fitness mini-goals. These will help you achieve your main goal, with ways to accomplish each mini goal. Mini goals will help you feel the success of your hard work, in the midst of striving towards your main goal.

❖ *Mini Goal #4:* _____

_____

○ _____
_____

○ _____
_____

❖ *Mini Goal #5:* _____

_____

○ _____
_____

○ _____
_____

❖ *Mini Goal #6:* _____

_____

○ _____
_____

○ _____
_____

Marriage & Relationship

Goals

~ Marriage & Relationship Goals Note Page ~

~Marriage & Relationship Goals~

MAIN GOAL (Mission Statement): _____

_____

_____

_____

❖ *Area of Focus for the Year*

    o   Keeping in mind the Fruits of the Spirit, Galatians 5:22 – 23, a wonderful place to start is focusing on the love, joy, peace, forbearance, kindness, goodness, faithfulness, gentleness, and self-control between your spouse and you. If you aren't married yet, it's a good time to start prioritizing your relationship with him/her before saying "I do."

    o   I'll dedicate time, energy and Prayer to focus on the _____ (and _____ _____) between myself and my spouse. I left an opening for those want to pick two.

❖ *Ways I Can Achieve This Goal*

    o   SMALL Things I Can do Each Day

        ▪ _____

        ▪ _____

        ▪ _____

        ▪ _____

    o   BIG Things I Can do Once a Week or Month

        ▪ _____

        ▪ _____

        ▪ _____

~ Marriage & Relationship Goals Note Page ~

Time to set your marriage and relationship mini-goals. These will help you achieve your main goal, with ways to accomplish each mini goal. Mini goals will help you feel the success of your hard work, in the midst of striving towards your main goal.

❖ Mini Goal #1: _____

_____

    ○ _____

       _____

    ○ _____

       _____

❖ Mini Goal #2: _____

_____

    ○ _____

       _____

    ○ _____

       _____

❖ Mini Goal #3: _____

_____

    ○ _____

       _____

    ○ _____

       _____

Parenting

Goals

~ Parenting Goals Note Page ~

~PARENTING GOALS~

MAIN GOAL (Mission Statement): _____

_____

_____

_____

❖ *Area of Focus for the Year*
- Proverbs 22:6 tells us to "train up" our children in the way they should go, so when they are old, they will have a solid foundation and not depart from this teaching.

- I'll dedicate time, energy and Prayer to focus on the _____

    _____ (and _____) between myself and my spouse. I left an opening for those want to pick two.

❖ *Ways I Can Achieve This Goal*
- SMALL Things I Can do Each Day

    - _____

    - _____

    - _____

- BIG Things I Can do Once a Week or Month

    - _____

    - _____

    - _____

~ Parenting Goals Note Page ~

Time to set your parenting mini-goals. These will help you achieve your main goal, with ways to accomplish each mini goal. Mini goals will help you feel the success of your hard work, in the midst of striving towards your main goal.

❖ *Mini Goal #1:* _____

_____

        ○ _____

        ○ _____

_____

❖ *Mini Goal #2:* _____

_____

        ○ _____

        ○ _____

_____

❖ *Mini Goal #3:* _____

_____

        ○ _____

        ○ _____

_____

Emotional

Photograph by Lisa M Buske
http://LisaMBuske.com

Goals

~ Emotional Goals Note Page ~

~EMOTIONAL GOALS~

MAIN GOAL (Mission Statement): _____

_____

_____

_____

❖ *Area of Focus for the Year:* Is there one aspect of life that you find more

difficult to maintain a healthy balance? _____

_____

    o Or that causes you more stress than others? Why do you think this

      is? Is it something you can control? _____

      _____

      _____

    o How does this affect your emotional state in relation to a "normal"

      routine? Why do think this is? _____

      _____

      _____

❖ *How do I set a goal for my emotions when our emotions are so*

unpredictable? I'm not an expert but through personal experience I've

learned it's important to first identify where our weakness is before we can

move forward. For instance, an emotional goal for me might be, "I will let the

words and actions of others go, rather than carrying a burden I'm not meant

to." A mini-goal for this goal could be, "I will pray about a situation before

speaking and interjecting my opinion."

~ Emotional Goals Note Page ~

Time to set your emotional mini-goals. These will help you achieve your main goal, with ways to accomplish each mini goal. Mini goals will help you feel the success of your hard work, in the midst of striving towards your main goal.

❖ *Mini Goal #1:* _____

_____

      ○   _____

           _____

      ○   _____

           _____

❖ *Mini Goal #2:* _____

_____

      ○   _____

           _____

      ○   _____

           _____

❖ *Mini Goal #3:* _____

_____

      ○   _____

           _____

_____

_____

~ Emotional Goals Note Page ~

❖ *Mini Goal #4:* _____

_____

_____

    ○ _____

       _____

    ○ _____

       _____

❖ *Mini Goal #5:* _____

_____

_____

    ○ _____

       _____

    ○ _____

       _____

❖ *Mini Goal #6:* _____

_____

_____

    ○ _____

       _____

    ○ _____

       _____

Financial

Goals

~ Financial Goals Note Page ~

~ FINANCIAL GOALS ~

❖ *What part of your finances will you target this year?* These are in no particular order, I brainstormed different areas we should focus based on books I've read or workshops attended. One thing I've learned, our financial journey and goals vary from each person to the next. If you are married, consult with your spouse to align your final goals.

- o *Tithe (start or increase)*
- o *Start or Increasing Savings Account Balance*
- o *Investing*
- o *Preparing for Retirement*
- o *Eliminating Debt*
- o *Controlling the Spending*
- o *Developing a Budget*
- o *A plan and prayer for God's wisdom, discernment, and will-power to set a goal and keep it.*

Now that you've thought about different areas of your finances, it's time to set at least one mail goal and mini-goals to achieve it. You may want to pick more than one, I've allowed space for

MAIN GOAL (Mission Statement): _____

_____

_____

_____

~ Financial Goals Note Page ~

Time to set your financial mini-goals. These will help you achieve your main goal, with ways to accomplish each mini goal. Mini goals will help you feel the success of your hard work, in the midst of striving towards your main goal.

❖ **Mini Goal #1:** _____

_____

    ○ _____

        _____

    ○ _____

        _____

❖ **Mini Goal #2:** _____

_____

    ○ _____

        _____

    ○ _____

        _____

❖ **Mini Goal #3:** _____

_____

    ○ _____

        _____

        _____

        _____

~ Financial Goals Note Page ~

❖ *Mini Goal #4:* _____

_____

_____

    ○   _____

              _____

    ○   _____

              _____

❖ *Mini Goal #5:* _____

_____

_____

    ○   _____

              _____

    ○   _____

              _____

❖ *Mini Goal #6:* _____

_____

_____

    ○   _____

              _____

    ○   _____

              _____

Reading

Goals

~ Reading Goals Note Page ~

~ READING GOALS ~

MAIN GOAL (Mission Statement): _____

_____

_____

_____

❖ *Possible Genres to Read From This Year:*

    ○ _____

    ○ _____

    ○ _____

    ○ _____

    ○ _____

❖ How Many Non-Fiction Books will You Read This Year? _____

❖ How Many Fiction Books will you Read This Year? _____

❖ How Many Books for Spiritual Growth will you Read This Year? ____

❖ Will you join a Book Club This Year? Or Possibly Lead One? _____

Business

Goals

~ Business Goals Note Page ~

~BUSINESS GOALS~

MAIN GOAL (Mission Statement) #1: _____

_____

_____

_____

Ways I Can Achieve This Goal

❖ *Mini Goal #1:* _____

_____

    ○   _____

        _____

    ○   _____

        _____

        _____

❖ *Mini Goal #2:* _____

_____

    ○   _____

        _____

    ○   _____

        _____

~ Business Goals Note Page ~

~BUSINESS GOALS~

MAIN GOAL (Mission Statement) #2: _____

_____

_____

_____

Ways I Can Achieve This Goal

❖ Mini Goal #1: _____

_____

     ○ _____

_____

     ○ _____

_____

❖ Mini Goal #2: _____

_____

     ○ _____

_____

     ○ _____

_____

~ Business Goals Note Page ~

~Business Goals~

MAIN GOAL (Mission Statement) #3: _____

_____

_____

_____

Ways I Can Achieve This Goal

❖ *Mini Goal #1:* _____

_____

○ _____

○ _____

_____

❖ *Mini Goal #2:* _____

_____

○ _____

○ _____

_____

Miscellaneous

& Personal

Goals

~ Miscellaneous & Personal Goals Note Page ~

MAIN GOAL (Mission Statement) #1: _____

_____

_____

_____

Ways I Can Achieve This Goal

❖ *Mini Goal #1:* _____

_____

    ○ _____

       _____

    ○ _____

       _____

❖ *Mini Goal #2:* _____

_____

    ○ _____

       _____

    ○ _____

       _____

~ Miscellaneous & Personal Goals Note Page ~

~MISCELLANEOUS & PERSONAL GOALS~

MAIN GOAL (Mission Statement) #2: _____

_____

_____

_____

Ways I Can Achieve This Goal

❖ *Mini Goal #1:* _____

_____

    ○ _____

        _____

    ○ _____

        _____

❖ *Mini Goal #2:* _____

_____

    ○ _____

        _____

    ○ _____

        _____

~ Miscellaneous & Personal Goals Note Page ~

~MISCELLANEOUS & PERSONAL GOALS~

MAIN GOAL (Mission Statement) #3: _____

_____

_____

_____

Ways I Can Achieve This Goal

❖ *Mini Goal #1:* _____

_____

    ○ _____

_____

    ○ _____

_____

❖ *Mini Goal #2:* _____

_____

    ○ _____

_____

    ○ _____

_____

I hope this journey of goal setting inspires and motivates you to be the best person you can by and possibly strive for more than you thought was possible before starting.

Please share you success with friends, family, and possibly me. One way we are more successful is with an accountability partner and sharing our accomplishments with like-minded individuals.

Visit my website: http://LisaMBuske.com and look for the Goal Tab to encourage others and be encouraged yourself.

Thank you again and I'm excited for you as you become the man or woman of God you are designed to be. Remember, there isn't a failed goal, just one in need of revision or redefining. You've got this!

www.ingramcontent.com/pod-product-compliance
Lightning Source LLC
Chambersburg PA
CBHW080154070426
42447CB00036B/3270